A Pocket Guide

Top Tips for Authors

by Penny Legg

SABRESTORM
STORIES

Designed and typeset by Ian Bayley.

British Library Cataloguing in Publication Data
A catalogue record for this book is available from the British Library

Published by Sabrestorm Stories Ltd., The Olive Branch, Caen Hill, Devizes, Wiltshire SN10 1RB United Kingdom. Company number 11927154.

Website: www.sabrestormstories.com
Email: enquiries@sabrestormstories.co.uk

ISBN 978-1-913163-02-0

Contents

Acknowledgements

No one writes a book in isolation and I am no exception. I would like to thank the following for their help and support during this book's journey to publication. Thank you, everyone!

Ian Bayley, my partner at Sabrestorm Stories, who thought the idea of a book of tips for authors was a good one, and who kept asking me if it was ready. It is now, Ian.

Dr Alison Baverstock and Emma Tait MA at Kingston University, London, my tutors on the MA Publishing course there. Remember the book I pitched for my assignment? Here it is!

Christine Donovan, Rubery Book Award Winner and Writing Buddy, who loved and endorsed my book. Thank you!

Simon Whaley, who showed me the way. Huge hugs, Simon.

My clients and friends over the years, including the lively writers at Writing Buddies; the writers at the charity Age Concern's writing programme in Southampton; Christine Kloser, Carrie Jareed and the lovely team at Capucia Publishing, and the many writers from all over the world who have asked me questions on writing courses, programmes and events where I was teaching. You have made me think about the information authors should know to allow them to move forward with their writing.

Last, but by no means least, my husband Joe, who spins plates behind the scenes so I can write.

In memory of my friend Jimmy, who first taught me that not all authors know what they need to know when writing for publication.

"How pleasant it is, at the end of the day,
No follies to have to repent;
But reflect on the past, and be able to say,
That my time has been properly spent."

Rhymes for the Nursery (1806) 'The Way to be Happy'
Ann Taylor (1782 – 1866) and Jane Taylor (1783 – 1824)
English writers of books for children

Introduction

Over the course of years as an author writing books, and as a coach working with countless beginner and more experienced wordsmiths, I have come to realise that most writers pick up knowledge piecemeal, a little here and a little there. This can lead to confusion, misinformation, and a lack of confidence for the writer, who, perhaps, does not wish to lose face by asking what might be seen as a naïve question. They are then embarrassed by their lack of knowledge and this puts them on the defensive. Often, too, writers do not know what they do not know.

If this strikes a chord, then this book is for you.

After marriage, a family and an on-going career as a journalist and author, I decided it was time to go back to university and fill in some of the blanks I had about one area of the business of writing. In 2017, I enrolled at Kingston University, London, on the MA Publishing course there. Stepping across the divide between writing and publishing was an eye-opener.

For nearly nine years I ran a support group for writers, Writing Buddies, which was based in Southampton, on the English south coast. This group, for beginners and professionals, offered support and advice on all aspects of the writing business. I was sad to close the group, which had some notable successes, but I was getting busier and there was no one else to step into my shoes. Between 2016 and 2024, I was an Author Coach for a US publishing concern, assisting authors in groups and in one-to-one meetings. I worked with leading UK charities for the retired to establish creative writing programmes, and have spoken at writing festivals on aspects of writing. Recently, I lectured on business writing at City, University of London and on journalism, creative writing, and media research at the University of Portsmouth. What has been a common theme throughout is that every student I have come across, regardless of the genre in which they write, has basically the same problems and questions. It was this realisation that led me to the outline of this book when, as part of the 'Create' Module for the MA Publishing course, I was tasked with pitching a new publishing product, including producing a financial forecast and a business plan for it. Initially, I had no idea what to come up with for this assignment and I spent a few sleepless nights worrying about it. Then, I remembered the old writers' adage: write about what you know. My assignment piece has, essentially, evolved into the book you are now reading.

I asked myself what I had wanted to know when I started out and then compared that to the questions I am being asked as a teacher now. I looked to see if there were books out there that addressed the issues I listed. The answer was yes, there were instructional books available, but they seemed to be written primarily for novelists. I wanted to write a book that would be useful to writers of all genres, not just those specialising in one area. I also wanted to write a book that a reader could dip into when needed, not something that had to be started at the beginning and read to the end to understand the concepts discussed. It needed, too, to be accessible to all, not an academic volume, but a practical and useful addition to any author's bookshelf. I also knew that no single volume was going to cover everything, so this book is aimed at the topics I am most asked about. In writing this book, my hope is that it will be a suitable accompaniment to the services supplied by Sabrestorm Stories, the publishing company I set up with my friend and colleague Ian Bayley, after I graduated from Kingston University, London with a Masters in Publishing, with Distinction.

Each chapter in this book holds useful tips designed to help any writer. If you have read this far, then not only do I thank you for doing so, but I also advise you that the best thing to read after this introduction is the chapter on the area you are most concerned about. You will then have an instant answer, which I hope will be helpful to you.

I wish you happy writing.

Penny Legg MA, BA(Hons), AFHEA, PTLL

"A work of art has no importance whatever to society. It is only important to the individual, and only the individual reader is important to me."

Strong Opinions (1973) p. 33
Vladimir Nabokov (1899 – 1977) Russian Novelist

Chapter 1
Know Your Audience

Who is your reader?

If writing for publication, the reader should be the most important person in the author's life. This is quite a bold statement but, if you take a moment to think about it, you will see that it is true. Without the reader to read the words, they are pointless.

Many books fail because the author has not thought about the needs of their reader when planning and writing it. This is often because the author is not sure who will be reading the book. However, consider this: if you, the author of the book, do not know who the book is aimed at, how can anyone else?

All writing, regardless of genre, needs to target someone. The best way to approach this is to try to think of a real person to focus on as you write, or at least a type of person. In this way, you can anticipate how they might think and react to your work.

Asking yourself some questions about your ideal reader is hugely useful in terms of identifying your audience. How old are they? What is their gender? What is their education, and their ethnicity? Are they in a relationship? Do they have children? Where do they shop? What do they do for a living? The more specific you can be, the better. These questions help to build up a picture of your reader that will sit in the back of your mind as you write. Better still, print the details out and put them on a nearby notice board so you can refer to them if you forget. This person, real or mythical, is so important that they will influence the way you write your book. The more you know about them, the easier it will be to write for them.

For example, suppose I wanted to write a children's storybook about adventurous kittens. Who might my reader be? Who is likely to want to read about the exploits of small, cute, cuddly bundles of fluff? I might decide that a little girl between five and seven years of age may be most interested in my kitten stories. She lives at home with her mother and little brother, in an inner-city flat where she cannot have pets, so reads about animals while imagining that she has one. Can you see how these decisions could influence the way I write the book? My choice of story, the language I use and the settings I invent should all be geared towards my mythical little reader, who might not yet be able to read the entire book by herself.

What does your reader want?

Knowing exactly what the reader is looking for in what you write and keeping this firmly in your mind as you work, will save you much time later. You will know immediately, for example, if your reader will not be able to follow a concept or if your language is too difficult to understand.

Following from this, your reader also influences the choice of topic or angle to write on. If you want to make book sales, for example, a prudent author will look at what is popular in the area they wish to write about. An online search will show which topics are more important to readers. For example, perhaps you want to write about gardening and are dithering about which subject to explore in your book. A gardening book giving general hints and tips, on the face of it, might have a wider audience appeal than a more focused book on a topic like container gardening. However, if you were planning a series of books, a general gardening book may not fit with readers looking for specialised content. A book exploring container gardening in more depth, for example, may be a better option in the long run, especially if you wrote books on greenhouse gardening and raised bed gardening, too. Readers would be more likely to think of you as a credible source of information on the general subject of 'gardening' if you wrote three specialised titles rather than a general one.

As an author, then, you need to know what your readers want to be able to cater to their needs. Taking this idea further, it follows that if you know your audience well enough, you will know whether what you are writing will be of interest to your reader. Writing a book about the history of the land your house is built upon is all very well, but will others be as enthusiastic? You do not want to waste your time on a topic that only interests you.

The audience for your work is tremendously important. Here are some tips to help when considering your reader:

- Take time to think about who your reader is. The more time you spend on them before you start writing, the better you will be able to serve their needs.

- Try to build up as complete a picture of your reader as possible. The more detail you have about them, the better you will understand them.

- Consider the angle your reader needs before you start writing. Getting this wrong will lead to frustration for you and your reader.

"What we call the start is often the end
And to make an end is to make a beginning.
The end is where we start from."

Four Quartets 'Little Gidding' (1942) pt. 5
T. S Eliot (Thomas Stearns Eliot) (1888 – 1965) Anglo-American Poet, Critic, and Playwright

Chapter 2
Getting Started

Where to start?

This is the question that worries the hard-pressed author who knows in their head what they want to say but does not quite know how to go about actually saying it.

As an author coach, I have this question asked often in one-to-one and in group sessions. The author usually has a lot of content, or several topics they want to write about, but does not know which to focus on.

Planning

Many authors start writing without any kind of plan for their work. They sit at their computer, or with pen poised, and begin without quite knowing where their words will lead them. Whilst I am sure that this method works for some, there is the danger that it can lead to disjointed, rambling prose, or to the author running aground because they do not know where they are going. They lose the point and end up writing into a corner. To avoid this, and to get organised, the author needs to plan their work. This is the first step towards answering the initial question.

At the beginning of each book there is often a Table of Contents. This is a section dedicated to telling the reader what to expect in the book, and where to find it. Depending on the subject, it may be as simple as a list of titled chapters and the page number in the book to look it up, or it could be a list of chapters with detailed sub-headings so that readers can search for sub-topics within the main theme of the chapter. If you look at my Table of Contents for this book, you will see that I have tried to keep my contents list as simple as possible, in keeping with the over-arching theme of the book, which is to offer tips to make life easier for authors. This theme stretches to being able to find areas of concern within the book, too. So, if you peep at my Table of Contents, you will find that it includes:

- a title – there is no doubt that the reader has found the Table of Contents;

- a titled list of the contents in a logical order;

- sub-headings to help the reader narrow down the search for particular information;

- the page number for each entry.

All but the page numbers can be planned at the beginning of the writing process. The page numbers will come after typesetting the text into a format ready for publication.

I love low-tech when initially planning the content for my writing. I find a notepad and pen, a glass of vino and a quiet spot, and think about all the various aspects of the topic. I write them all down in a list, adding things as I think of them. If I have problems, which happens sometimes, I use a spidergram. This is so-called because it resembles a spider's web when completed. This allows me to add sub-headings to main themes and lets me see at a glance what content I have come up with for each and any subjects where I did not have sufficient material. This allows me to make decisions about what finally to take forward into the book and what to leave for another time. The spidergram for this book is on page 19, complete with authentic spelling error!

Some people use index cards to note topics for their work and keep putting ideas on individual cards until they feel that they have enough to fill a book. Other writers use computer programmes, such as Microsoft Excel, Google Sheets or Trello, to keep track of their ideas. There is no need to worry about how you do it,

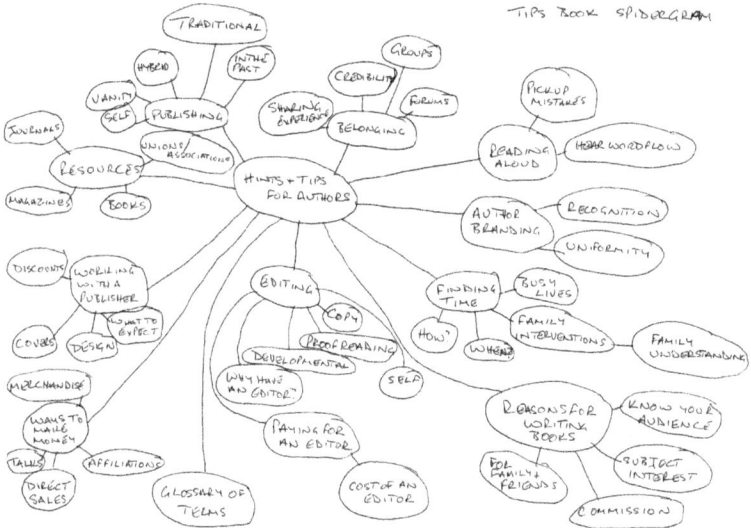

the point is to get the ideas in your head out into the world so that they can then be organised into a logical sequence for the document being written. Thus, for example, as you can see from my spidergram, when I was thinking about this book, I had lots of areas in my initial brainstorm, some of which eventually made it to the book.

Once you have all the topics you feel you could cover, you need to consider how best to do so. Looking objectively at the areas in your list will reveal some ideas that naturally link. If you physically put them together you are starting to build your chapters. Thus, in this book, for example, I decided to write one chapter about editing. Many writers do not understand the different types of editing, what is involved and whether it is worth the expense to hire a professional editor to work on their manuscript. As this is the case, making the decision to include this topic in the book was a no-brainer. Thus, my headings for this theme were Editing as the chapter title, and then the different types of editing became sub-headings within that chapter. When I looked at these logically, I found a chronological sequence that made sense: developmental editing first, followed by copy and line-editing and then proofreading.

I hope you can see from this exercise that by detailed planning like this, I was building the Table of Contents. This became, essentially, the backbone of my book. As I wrote, I could amend the list by moving chapters up or down, or by adding to or deleting sub-headings. I could see at a glance what I had decided to write about and where that text fitted into the overall structure of the book.

Writing

With all of this decided, it is time to move on to the second part of answering the 'where to start' question. This involves writing the work.

You can start writing where you like within your overall framework. There is no hard and fast rule. Some authors begin at the beginning with the introduction, proceed through all the headings and sub-headings in order and arrive at the bibliography happy writers. Others, like me, jump about. They take a topic from the list and spend time writing about it before slotting it into the script and then selecting another topic to work on. Only at the end of their work do they look back on the completed whole. The point is that each author can make an informed decision as to where to start because they can see at a glance from their list what there is to write about. It is just a question of which topic to choose to write on in that session. This puts the author in charge of the work, rather than the work taking charge of the author and possibly leading them into a corner.

I have concentrated on book writing here but building a structure to follow is equally useful no matter what kind of document you are writing. A list of contents will keep you on the straight and narrow, avoid you going off at a writing tangent and will save you time and effort in the long run. Writing to topic takes the pressure off the author and leads to more writers fully finishing their writing project rather than coming to a halt halfway, or worse, not starting because of not knowing where to begin.

Here are some tips to help get you started:

- The more detailed your planning, the easier it will be to write as you will have a guide to keep you from going off at a tangent.

- Once you begin writing, remember, just write. Do not worry about anything other than emptying the contents of your brain onto the page. Tidying it all up can be done later!

Good luck!

"Time's thievish progress to eternity."

Sonnet 77
William Shakespeare (1564 – 1616) English Playwright

Chapter 3
Finding Time

The problem of finding time to write is a sticky one. We all start with good intentions. "We will write every day," we say, piously. We give ourselves quotas and swear we will produce a set number of words each session. We clear a space on our dining room table or on the spare bedroom dressing table, or we create a home office in a cubbyhole under the stairs or the elastic guest room, so we are ready for the off. We spread the word that we are going to be writing each day so that, in theory at least, we are undisturbed while working. We then breathe a sigh of relief that all is ready, and we set to, full of enthusiasm.

This is when the realities of life start to appear. Everyone in the household knows you are working at home, which is great for them when they need a parcel delivery signed for or a child minded for an hour or two. If a family member is sick, there is a built-in nurse. The household pet realises you are there more than usual and so takes advantage by demanding attention. They already know which desk drawer the treats are in, so they make a beeline to it and will not stop scratching at it until they get what they want. I speak from experience. Sigh.

Author and publisher, Ian Bayley, points out other areas that catch writers unawares. "Turn the phone off!" he advises. This is such a simple thing to do but how many writers think to do it? Each time it rings we automatically answer and then we are lost. "The biggest distraction in the universe is the internet," Ian continues. "Before you know it, you spend three hours on YouTube!" How many writers are guilty of this timewaster? Hmm…

Distractions soon start to dent your resolve – and your word count. So, what can you do to balance the demands of everyday life with your need to write and keep to a schedule? After all, you might have a deadline to meet. If this is the case, there will probably be penalties imposed for late delivery.

The answer is not easy and different authors tackle it in different ways.

The first thing to realise is that you cannot be everything to everyone and continue to heap pressure on yourself by being Super Writer! You need to be realistic and practical. If you have a grandchild to look after for two hours a day, build that into your schedule.

The odd fifteen minutes

Look for pockets of time when you know you will be able to work – early in the morning, perhaps, or late at night. It might be, when you really look at what you have going on in your life, that you have much less time to write than you realised. That is okay, though. It is the realisation that is key here. Once you take stock and understand that your dream of writing all day, every day was just that, a dream, you can start to work out what you really can do, and when. So, what are you doing at lunch time? If you are in a job where you have thirty minutes for lunch, could you use half of this time to write something? Or research something? Or plan something? In other words, could you usefully employ this small amount of time to keep yourself working? If the answer is yes, then you will have successfully found a pocket to exploit.

Finding half an hour

Getting up half an hour before usual is often a profitable move. This period is likely to be quiet, especially if you shut the door on Fido and resolutely keep it shut. What do you usually do with the half hour after your grandchild goes home? Tidy up? Make a cup of coffee and get your breath back? Either way, this is valuable time. Why not tidy up later and take your coffee to your desk?

My point is that there are often small parcels of time in the day that we all overlook when trying to find time to write. Look for these, make a note of them and then use them. Make sure that you are disciplined and take steps to ensure you do use them. No matter how small the amount of time, if you use that time whenever you have it, you will see your writing progress.

Longer spells

Looking for longer spells of time requires dedication. It might also take more than just a quick re-evaluation of your day-to-day routine.

One option is to look at the routines of others in your household. Does your partner work shifts or have a regular commitment out of the home, for example? If so, this really does open opportunity for your writing. Look for periods when they are working or away from home during which you would normally not work. For example, if your other half works in the evening would you usually fill in some of that time with a glass of wine and a movie while waiting for them to come home? If so, think about this. The average movie is nearly two hours long. Five evenings out working is equal to ten hours of time. Why not make a point of using some or all these sessions to write? I appreciate that you might have caring responsibilities or your own outside commitments during this time, but even if you managed one session a week, it is two hours of productive time. Just think what you could do with that!

Similarly, is there scope for extra time becoming available at the weekend because of your partner's work patterns? If there is any time here when you would normally not work because you want quality time with your partner, but cannot do so because they are not there, then seize the opportunity! For example, if your partner works one Saturday morning in four, then hey, presto! If the kids are playing sport and you are just there as their taxi driver, take a notebook, a voice recorder or your laptop with you and use the waiting time profitably. If you are offered some unexpected childcare, take it and then get writing!

Just be ready to spot the chance for extra writing time when it appears.

The Retreat

For longer periods of dedicated writing time, there is always the retreat.

A writers' retreat is exactly what it sounds like – an opportunity to retreat from everyday life completely and to spend your time writing. This offers dedicated time to work in. A retreat is usually something you opt into, joining other like-minded writers who are seeking the time and space to think about and work on their project without the stress of their usual commitments.

Some opt for virtual writing retreats. These are sessions where writers meet up virtually, perhaps using an online meeting app, at a set time. They share details of their project and what they hope to accomplish during the retreat, and then go away to write for a given period of time. At the end of that time, they meet virtually once more and share their successes. Virtual writing retreats have the advantage that they are usually relatively inexpensive compared to other types of retreat and can be set up easily as they are held totally online. They are morale boosting and usually produce focused results.

The opposite of a virtual writing retreat is an in-person retreat.

An organised in-person retreat involves writers congregating at a venue for a set number of days. It may be a weekend, a mid-week break, a week or longer. The participants use that time to work on their project. This kind of retreat offers a degree of sociability as writers meet for meals and may spend their evenings communally, either discussing their project or doing something completely different from writing, like playing games or walking. The advantage of in-person writing retreats is that there are no distractions. You pay (often quite a large amount) for peace and quiet, a physical place to write (a desk, chair etc) and ambiance conducive to allowing words to flow. The fee will usually include full-board and lodging and may also include events like author talks or feedback sessions on your work. Organised writing retreats are popular and are often a pleasant way for a writer to find time to write, as well as have a change of scene and to meet new people. Many writers book an organised retreat as their annual holiday.

Some writers belong to writing circles, which organise their own retreats. These are often in rented houses, chosen because they are in a location that is peaceful and that might have options for walking or sightseeing nearby. Group members know each other, and the trip is a chance to share work with trusted colleagues. The group decides when they will write and will congregate for meals, which they cook themselves. In-person retreats like this are often fun and eagerly anticipated.

I am not suggesting that finding time for writing is easy. Here are some tips to help you find the time you need to complete your project:

- Think practically about the commitments you have and plan your writing around any you cannot change.

- Do not underestimate the power of a short writing session. If you are organised, you will achieve more than you might assume.

- Seize the moment! Use any unexpected time offered you.

- Be disciplined and always try to write when you have planned to do so.

- Ask your nearest and dearest not to interrupt you when you are writing.

Finding Time to Write

I remember how a new author came to me determined to write her book in less than six months and was full of plans about how she was going to get it written in that time. The subject was quite complex, and I did wonder if she had set herself a realistic deadline, particularly as she aimed to write about 85,000 words, but, she knew her topic, so I crossed my fingers.

At first, all was okay. She wrote for several hours four days a week and produced about 12,000 words in the first month. This would have given her 72,000 words in six months. A little short, but she was hopeful she could make up the difference as she went along. She was very excited. I was pleased for her.

Then, little by little, her wordcount started to slip as small things got in the way. Pretty soon it was obvious, to me at least, that finishing by deadline was not going to happen. Reality hit for her when she wrote the following to me. Bless her, it was a hard lesson.

'In between taking the dog to the vet, babysitting my grandson, nipping to the shops and cooking dinner, I wrote 300 words today!'

"Reading is to the mind what exercise is to the body."

The Tatler no. 147 (18 March 1710)
Sir Richard Steel (1672 – 1729) Irish-born Essayist and Playwright

Chapter 4
Reading Aloud

It is easy to spot a manuscript that has not been read aloud. It is full of errors, both in grammar and in spelling. It may sound stilted or contain difficult to read words, and the content might be jumbled and without a logical flow. Any, or all, of these areas point to a work written in a hurry by an over-eager writer. A script presented in this manner does not show the author, or the resulting composition, in a good light.

Reading aloud is such a simple thing to do and is so useful, but how many writers do it before launching their baby out into the world? The answer is, not enough. By missing this vital step, they are letting themselves down, probably ruining their chances of acceptance and publication, and they end up dejected and sad after (another) rejection.

If this sounds a bit dramatic, it is because it is!

Why read aloud?

So, why is reading a script aloud so important?

Well, your eyes and brain play a trick on you. As you read silently to yourself, your brain fills in for mistakes your eyes skim over, such as spelling errors or missing words, so you are fooled into thinking that all is well with your work. Your brain knows what you thought you were writing and tells you that you did, actually, do so. It is only when you introduce a third dimension, your voice, that things go wrong. All of a sudden, you are speaking what is on the page and this forces you to confront all the errors your eyes and brain have been at pains to shield you from. Now, you can 'see' the mistakes, warts and all. This can be painful. You wonder how on earth you omitted letters, wrote some words twice, spelt everything in American instead of British English etcetera. Wince!

Reading aloud may be embarrassing, especially if you are doing so in front of others in the office or at the kitchen table, but it is necessary. In an age where there are so many writers competing for publication, whether traditionally or with a hybrid publisher, no writer can be complacent. It is a sad fact that too many mistakes kill work. They show a lack of care and pride in the manuscript. If it is a book, a traditional publisher will reject it unless there is some other, compelling, reason to take it on. If it is an article, a credible newspaper or magazine will reject, too, because they expect professionally written and presented prose. If you have invested in support as you write, an author coach or an editor will flag up the mistakes and help sort them out, proving the worth of spending money on them. Often though, the writer is left with a good idea ruined by simply not reading the work aloud before sending it out into the world.

How to Read Aloud

It is not just a case of intoning each word and mindlessly repeating what is on the screen or page. No, it is much more than that. Yes, each word needs to be spoken but all the punctuation should be read with the words. Thus, if there is a comma, for example, do not rush over the text. Pause … and then read on. This gives the script the emphasis that the punctuation calls for.

If you stumble, there is a problem. You have not faltered for nothing. As soon as you detect a problem, stop and remedy the cause. Even if you cannot see the mistake immediately, keep looking at the text, re-reading it aloud until what is causing you to waver becomes evident. There will be something – a word out of place, perhaps, or maybe it has slipped into the wrong tense, the past, perhaps, when it should be in the present. Once you have found the cause of the stumble, play with your words until you find the form that flows.

Do not rush. Read slowly. It is not a race to the finish. You are looking for areas that disrupt, interrupt, hold up or are unclear, so take time to find them. By reading the text aloud, areas of concern should pop out at you simply because you are forcing your brain and eyes to be responsible and report the truth.

Taking a few extra minutes to read your work aloud will pay dividends. It will be the last check that all is well and that the script is, in fact, ready to take flight. You will have the satisfaction of knowing that there is no chance of its being returned because of errors you have not taken the trouble to identify.

Here are some tips to help you to read aloud:

- Brush up on the rules of punctuation. This way, the knowledge is fresh in your mind and so you will be more likely to recognise a problem when you come across it – and will know what to do about it.

- Ignore anyone else in the room when you read aloud. Better yet, invite them to listen in. That way, you will have the added benefit of a second pair of ears to help find mistakes!

"The reader is more intolerant of mistakes than you may suspect."

The Naked Author - A Guide to Self-Publishing (2011) ch. 13
Alison Baverstock, Professor of Publishing and Director of the Kingston University Big Read, with Margaret Aherne, a founder member of the Chartered Institute of Editing and Proofreading

Chapter 5
Editing and Editors

Editing your own work

When we write, we automatically monitor what we are saying, picking up obvious errors as we go along. Then, when we have our first draft ready, we go through it looking for areas that we have missed, sections we want to re-write or grammatical problems to correct. We may produce several versions of our text as we hone it to perfection.

A Cautionary Tale

Once upon a time, there was a writer who loved to write. She wrote and wrote, filling pages with her words. She wrote first thing in the morning before she had her breakfast, after her bowl of cereal and mug of coffee, after lunch and into the evening every day. She was inspired! She was on fire! She had ideas and they dripped from her fingers as she scribbled away. She was happy. Then, one day, she thought she would look back at what she had written. She had not finished what she was writing but, she reasoned, what could be the harm in just having a quick peep at all those lovely words already on the pages? So, she stopped writing. Her new ideas stopped flowing as she gave her attention instead to all the ideas she had already put down on paper. She read and read. It was exciting to see all the work she had done but, as she read, she found that some of the words did not sound quite as good as they had when she wrote them. She immediately started working on them to make them better. Beginning at the very first sentence, she went through each line, one by one, making changes as she went. She found that she had made a great many mistakes and soon felt sad at how much she had to change. Her happiness with her work dimmed but she was determined to press on and make what she had written the best it could be. When she got to the end of her work, she was happy again. Now it was edited, it could be read properly. Just to make sure it was okay, and she had not missed anything, she went back to the beginning and started reading through once more, red pen poised in hand, just in case. Pretty soon, she read a passage that did not sound quite as she thought it had and so she stopped to edit it. Then, a few lines down, she found something else to work on. Soon, she was deeply into editing the manuscript for a second time. However, she was not daunted. She knew it had to be the best it could be and so she ploughed on to the end. During the night, she dreamt about what she had written and went over it in her mind. She soon realised that there were a couple of passages that would not do. They would need to be revised when she was back at her desk. Sure enough, as soon as she sat down in her office, she started editing the offending sections again. By now, all the baby ideas that had been bobbing about in her brain, waiting for their time to be born and to blossom, gave up waiting and vanished. All her excitement about the new work disappeared and she found herself stuck in a never-ending cycle of edit and re-edit. Sadly, this is where we leave her. She will never finish her manuscript because she has lost the impetus to do so and all her ideas and enthusiasm have gone. All that early promise has vanished. What is left is worth nothing because it is incomplete.

The moral of this tale is that you must finish your manuscript before you start editing it. Do not be like our heroine and get lost in a sea of never-ending edits!

Here are some of my top tips to ensure you do edit but you do not edit endlessly. Remember, you want to finish with a piece of writing that is worth reading, so always keep your reader in mind as you go through this list.

- Never start editing until you have finished all you intend writing. As *A Cautionary Tale* demonstrates, it will kill creativity and mean that you will probably not finish writing the piece you are working on.

- When you finish a draft, put it in a drawer and leave it. Go and do something completely different. Give your mind a break. It is your baby and when you write it, you think it is perfect. This is completely understandable but invariably found to be wrong!

- Having given yourself time for the text to dim in your mind, when you look at it again, read it aloud. We discussed the value of doing this in Chapter Four. You will notice all manner of errors as you read and to do so will be a valuable first step in your editing process.

- Know when to stop editing. There must be a point when you call a halt. Recognise that you will probably have a professional editor look at your script and they will assist you with further editing work.

- Related to this, look for a natural ending point in your work. Often, there is one and it is overlooked. Look critically at what you have written and see if there is a point where you could naturally finish the text without compromising the integrity of what you have said. Go to this point and complete the manuscript there.

The Editor

Eventually comes the day we pass our baby over to one who has a professional eye for errors, an editor. Depending on your point of view, this can be either an exciting day, as your work is seen by an outsider for the first time, or a nerve-racking day, as you pluck up the courage to give your work to someone who is not so emotionally close to it. Either way, the time comes to most writers and it is a milestone event.

What do we mean when we talk about an 'editor'? Most of us know that we have a part to play in making text better. We need to be aware of what and how we write so that our words are the best they can be. What, in fact, does an editor do and is there more than one kind of editor? Are editors friends or foes to the average writer?

The Oxford English Dictionary defines 'Edit' as *"assemble, prepare, or modify (written material, especially the work of another or others) for publication".*

With this in mind, here are some of the different kinds of editing a writer will encounter and a little on what the editor actually does.

Developmental Editing

Developmental editing seeks to make sense of a writing project as a whole. The developmental editor tries to guide a writer. In a nutshell, the developmental editor may

- imagine a topic or area to write about;

- help with planning the work;

- assist the author to develop the project;

- and, if necessary, will instruct the author on the best way to proceed.

Developmental editing in book publishing is often the last resort when you have a piece of writing that needs substantial work to make it publishable.

Most writers cannot edit themselves apart from fixing obvious mistakes. This is because the work they are producing is too close to them. They know what they want to say and think that they have said it. So, any revision of the text is tainted with the knowledge that it is already 'good enough'. If you work with a developmental editor, they will propose other ways to look at your work, acting as a guide to get you to where your work needs to be.

They will think of the needs of the audience and help you to plan and execute your work in a manner that will create the best possible outcome for the most important person associated with written work – the person who buys and reads it. A developmental editor will consider questions, such as: Is the subject the best for your audience? If not, which aspect of it might be?

Developmental editors can help authors focus on their theme. Often, topics are huge and are too big to cover in one sitting. Writers do not always realise this. They do not break it down into smaller, more manageable chunks and start writing at the beginning, expecting to continue through to the end. Often, the writer then runs into a brick wall, which is caused by a lack of thought about the many and varied aspects of the subject. The dawning realisation is that the matter is bigger than they had thought and so they become overwhelmed. The resulting work is either incomplete or haphazard.

Stepping back and thinking logically and objectively about a subject is one aspect of developmental editing. What is the area of concern? What are the aspects of it that should be covered?

How can these be broken down so that they are manageable for the writer to write and logical for the reader to read them? The answers to these questions might be totally different to what the writer originally thought but it is important to realise that the writer is still the one in charge. Developmental editing will enhance the work, not take it over.

The developmental editor will also look at the planning of a piece of writing. Have you ever looked at a Table of Contents in a book? It is organised so that it is in a logical list for the reader.

This is the Table of Contents for my book on WW2 crime, *Crime in the Second World War: Spivs, Scoundrels, Rogues and Worse* (2017).

Contents
Acknowledgements
Foreword by Michael O'Bryne QPM, Chief Constable (Rtd), Bedfordshire Police
Introduction - Was There Crime in the Second World War?
Chapter 1 Looting
Chapter 2 The Black Market
Chapter 3 Crimes by Black Out
Chapter 4 Murder
Chapter 5 Fraud, Theft, Hooch and Other Crimes
Chapter 6 Armed Services Crime
Bibliography
Index

As you can see, it has all the traditional pieces you would expect of a book: I thank those who have helped with the writing of it; I have asked a reputable person to write the Foreword; there is an introductory section to lead the reader into the book and then there are chapters laid out in a common-sense sequence before a bibliography and an index, both designed to help the reader with further research or to navigate the book.

Now look at this Table of Contents:

Contents
Foreword by Michael O'Bannon, Police Constable,
    Metropolitan Police, 2010 - 2015
Introduction - Was There Crime in the Second World War?
Chapter - Armed Services Crime
Acknowledgements
Bibliography
Chapter – Murder
Chapter 3 Crimes by Black Out
Chapter - Looting
Chapter - The Black Market
Chapter - Fraud, Theft, Hooch, witchcraft, spying, looting,
    white collar crime
Bibliography
Index

This is different, isn't it? If this came before a developmental editor, they would have much to say about it!

To begin with, it is jumbled up and does not flow. The Foreword is written by an unknown, with only a short connection to the subject. The table has not been thought through and reads as if it has been listed as thoughts came to mind. The bibliography is mentioned twice. When developmentally editing this, it would be assembled into a logical order. The choice of person to write the Foreword might be questioned, perhaps with different options given for someone more prestigious and therefore more useful to the book. The result would be a coherent and flowing contents list.

My book had two chapters that might, on the face of it, contain information on one area of crime – murder. One of the decisions I had to make as an author was where to put the murder cases I was writing about – perhaps in the chapter on murder or perhaps in the chapter about service crime, those crimes committed by military personnel, as some of the murderers were in the armed forces at the time of the offences. However, a developmental editor might have suggested to me that some of these crimes would be better where they had a particular connection, perhaps in the chapter about the wartime blackout or when discussing the black market. Thus, when planning my work, I could have given due thought to the advice given to me by the developmental editor and changed my initial thoughts on the distribution of these entries.

By its very nature, developmental editing is about developing the text to be the best it can be. Suggestions for developing the text are made as a result of a thorough and ongoing appraisal of the work, and by getting to know it so well that it becomes second nature to the developmental editor. By standing back and taking stock of the overall work, the developmental editor can see through the emotions the text engenders within the writer. It is not their baby, so they can look at it objectively. They will understand your vision as an author and know what you hope to accomplish. In short, the developmental editor will help keep you to the point.

Working with a developmental editor is usually quite exciting! It can be revealing to realise how they see your work. They see the possibilities you might have overlooked. Some writers do find this intimidating, though. They see it as criticism and do not stop to reflect that what is advised comes from experience and a deep understanding of your project. A developmental editor wants the best for their client and will strive to ensure that the text is the best it can be. A writer needs to remember this when listening to the developmental editor's ideas. If they embrace them, it really can be rewarding!

Here are some tips and things to remember when working with a developmental editor:

- They understand your work as a reader. Why is this so important? The reader is the most important part of the whole process as without a reader there is no point to writing.

- They see the gaps, think about the options, bring them to the writer's attention and show possible ways forward.

- They are completely objective and so do not have an agenda when discussing the text. Their sole aim is to make the text the best it can be.

- It is morale-boosting to have someone on your side. We all have well-meaning friends and family who will tell you that everything you write is great. They do not want to hurt your feelings and so will tell you what you want to hear. This is not always helpful! An objective person on your side will tell you straight when things work and when they do not.

- They become part of your team. You are not alone anymore! Yay! This can be hugely useful.

- They will support and encourage you, getting you through difficult patches when perhaps your work is not flowing, and you do not know how to get it going again.

- Overall, the developmental editor will give you confidence. You will come away from the developmental editing experience feeling far happier with your work and the impact it will have on the reader.

Professional developmental editors are not cheap. They are paid well because they can fundamentally change a book for the best. I specify a book as this is the area that most people hire developmental editors to work in. However, developmental editing can apply to any type of written work.

Copy Editing

Copy editors work across all genres of writing, in books, magazines and other text. They make your words work for you. They do this by ensuring that written text is concise. You do not want to bore your reader with rambling prose, do you? If you fill a page with words that do nothing to move a story forward or do not paint a mental picture for your reader, they are just filler and should be weeded out. This can be tremendously difficult for some authors, who grow fond of favourite phrases. A copy editor will see through word fluff and cut to the heart of the text to make it say just what you want it to say, and no more.

More than this, though, a good copy editor will also make sure the text has a consistent style and tone overall. Style refers to the words and punctuation used and the way they are structured in terms of basics, such as headings, sentences, and paragraphs. There are several styles of writing. For example, if I were to write my children's book about adventurous kittens from Chapter One, I would use a style that is simple, clear, and engaging, with short words, sentences, and paragraphs. The story and how the child reading it will receive it would be the focus for me if I were writing this book. Academic, or scholarly, writing, on the other hand, employs a completely different style. Simple words are not necessarily useful in this kind of text. Instead, academic writing may be formal and structured. It will need to be clear to ensure that difficult or theoretical concepts are explained in terms that can be understood by the educated reader. This book, for example, employs an easy to read, conversational style. I want it to be read and understood by the widest range of readers, so

I have deliberately made style choices such as regular, bolded sub-headings, so that they act as signposts to readers looking for particular information on a topic quickly. I hope I have got to the point swiftly and that what I say is useful, clear, and concise. These are all stylistic choices made by the author, me.

Tone reflects how the author feels about the topic under discussion. Have you ever read a piece of writing and wondered if the author got out of bed on the wrong side that day? As a reader you pick up on the tone used by the writer, whether it be happy or sad, neutral, angry, or anxious. Tone comes out in vocabulary choices; the way sentences are structured, and the punctuation decisions made. Of course, what you are writing may influence the tone you use. If you are writing as an angry young person, for example, you will write using a different tone than if you were writing as an elderly woman looking back over her life with a sense of satisfaction.

A copy editor will notice when the style or tone changes and will correct it, or at least flag it up so that the author can rectify it. After all, if an aberrant author declines to effect change, it can affect the collective comprehension of the work. What? You see my point?!

Readers are not stupid and will notice mistakes quickly, so copy editors ensure that your manuscript is grammatically accurate and factually correct. These two editorial functions are important to note as errors here will do more to undermine your text than all other problems put together. Just imagine if your sentence read something like this:

Magna Carta was signed at Runneymede, just outside Windsor in Hampshire, in 1089.

On the face of it, all is well. There are no red wavy lines under any of the words on my screen, so my computer's spellchecker is happy. However, are all the component facts of the sentence correct? Was the Magna Carta, the Charter of Rights signed by King John of England, really signed at Runneymede? Is the place name correct, despite the lack of wavy lines? Is this near Windsor? Is Windsor in Hampshire? Is the stated date correct? All of these questions keep the copy editor busy and, in turn, means that the author's credibility remains intact as Windsor magically moves to Berkshire and the signing date becomes 1215.

The Copy Editor also ensures that each sentence is easy to read. This is an important and often overlooked area. Many writers think that if they can read it, then all readers will be able to do so. However, it is not quite as simple as that. If it is too difficult, you will lose your reader. If it is too easy, you might offend your readership and not be taken seriously. One way to ensure readability is to use the scale devised by Rudolf Franz Flesch (1911 – 1986) and J. Peter Kincaid (b. 1947) in the 1970s. The Flesch-Kincaid readability tests are designed to test how difficult a passage is to read in English. Originally developed for the US military, the pursuit of plain English has led the tests to be used widely and is a useful addition to many word processing packages, such as Word in Microsoft Office (where you will find it as part of Editor). The higher the readability score, the easier the text is to read. Thus, a score of 90 – 100 can be easily understood by an eleven-year-old and a score of 0 – 10 means that the text is so difficult that only someone with a university education will be able to read it. The average to aim for is a score between 60 and 70, which is the approximate standard a student would reach in Grade eight or nine in the US education system. This equates to an age range of between 13 and 15 years. A script at this level will be written to ensure readability by the maximum number of readers. This book, for example, has a readability score of 65.8 and a grade level of 8.4, meaning that everyone reading it will be able to understand it. Fab!

Here is a list of the Flesch-Kincaid Readability Scores and what they mean:

Score	School Level/Age	What This Means
100.0–90.0	5th grade/11 years	Very easy to read.
90.0–80.0	6th grade/12 years	Easy to read. Conversational English.
80.0–70.0	7th grade/13 years	Fairly easy to read.
70.0–60.0	8th to 9th grade/ 14 & 15 years	Plain English. The level to aim for.
60.0–50.0	10th to 12th grade/ 16 to 18 years	Fairly difficult to read.
50.0–30.0	College/University	Difficult to read.
30.0–10.0	College/ University graduate	Very difficult to read.
10.0–0.0	Professional	Extremely difficult to read.

(Adapted from the excellent overview table given on https://en.wikipedia.org/wiki/ Flesch%E2%80%93Kincaid_readability_tests under the following license: https://creativecommons. org/licenses/by-sa/3.0/)

Copy editors also ensure that the points expressed are in a logical, sequential manner. In other words, they flow smoothly from one to the next. There is nothing worse than trying to keep up with an author who jumps about, rather like a demented flea! Points should be made a step at a time so that readers can follow without difficulty, not thrown in willy-nilly for the reader to decipher, or not, as the case may be. You do not want readers to put the book down because they are confused or lost by the jumps in the text.

So, copy editing modifies and enhances written work. A good copy editor can make your text zing. Copy editing comes into play when you have a version of the manuscript that you are reasonably happy with, but you know that there are errors and inconsistencies. It might be a second or later version, perhaps after developmental editing work has taken place. Sometimes the work of the copy editor is common sense. No one wants to read verbose, long-winded prose and so the copy editor will look for this kind of problem. Being concise, in an age where attention spans are not long, is a useful skill.

Thus, if you want to confuse your reader, then write in an obscure way. If you want to give your reader an easy, understandable read, then copy edit!

Let us copy edit this passage for concision.

> **Ted ran across the road, trying not to stumble into the potholes as he had once before. His ankle was broken then and he remembered the pain he felt as he fell into the mud, which drenched his new, designer trousers, bought the day before, and how it had seeped into the lace holes of his brogues, a present from his girlfriend. The ground was hard as he hit it and small stones embedded themselves in his skin, making the sore points bleed. His ankle had hurt like hell. The ambulance crew said they knew it was broken as soon as they saw the red veins standing out on the swelling joint. He reached the other side and went into the pub.**

123 words

As you can see, there is much that has no useful purpose in the text, so could be omitted in the script to make it more concise and to move the action along. The reader does not need to know all the details about what happened to the character when he fell into a pothole in the past. They do not have anything to do with the current story and just serve to puff out the word count. Thus, they can safely be deleted without damaging the sense of action:

Ted ran across the road, trying not to stumble into the potholes as he went. He reached the other side and went into the pub.

25 words

Copy editing is about being able to spot problems in the text and often also includes line editing as an editor goes line by line inspecting every word and punctuation mark. Problems spotted might be a spelling mistake, a spacing error, an inaccurate statement, or something else entirely. Nowadays, copy editing is often undertaken directly into the text using a tool like Track Changes so that the author can see the changes indicated and make a decision as to whether to accept the edit, or not.

Here are some tips and areas to think about when working with an editor:

- Faster is not necessarily better. You do not want your editor to miss things, so allow them the time needed to edit properly. Be aware, though, that editors are human. They do make mistakes. This should not be held against them. Just remember all the problems they fixed along the way, not the odd one they missed.

- The cleaner the text, in other words, the fewer errors there are in it, the easier it should be to edit, but there may be specialist knowledge required to edit the book, which may slow down the process.

- Price is often an indicator of quality, as in most things! After giving a full brief, so your prospective editor knows exactly what you want, ask for an estimate in advance. Estimates will either be an amount per so many words (usually per word or per 1000 words) or an amount per hour. In the UK, the Chartered Institute of Editors and Proofreaders issues guidelines for the minimum amount per hour that editors and proofreaders charge. This information will give you a good idea of what you should expect to pay for an editor. There will be editors who charge less and there are editors who will charge considerably more. A recommendation from a trusted source is often useful.

Proofreading

'Proofreading' is often the term used erroneously as a catch-all for editing, full stop. A 'proof' is the shortened form of 'galley proof', which is the name given to the blown-up versions of each laid-out page that a publisher sends out to the author to be 'read' or checked before going to print.

Proofreading is the last chance to catch problems before the work goes into production. Nowadays, most proofreading takes place electronically, although if you have the option, you are likely to catch more mistakes on a hard copy than you are on a screen. Just staring at a screen can make your eyes tired and so you are more likely to miss an error.

When you are checking your proofs, it goes without saying that you should know your text. Errors should stand out, but it is a good idea to make sure that you can check areas such as spellings and acronyms are correct, with a dictionary or something similar, if necessary. Ensure you have refreshed your mind on any style guidance you have been issued, too.

It is important to give yourself time to do a thorough job. Remember, the next stage in your manuscript's life is the biggest one – the leap to publication. If you rush, you are more likely to miss errors. Good advice is always to allow yourself at least twice the time you think it will take you to proofread your work.

Much as we all love Fido or Tiddles, when you are proofreading, they are best kept in another room, preferably out of hearing range so you are not subject to bouts of guilt when you hear plaintive whining or mewing. This also goes for little Jenny or Johnny, too. Proofreading is best undertaken undisturbed as interruptions break concentration. So, turn off your mobile and log out of your emails, ask a significant other to take the dog for a walk or look after the children and then devote your entire attention to checking your proof. It really is that important. Mistakes are notoriously easy to miss.

Being able to cut and paste text from one programme to another is a real boon to designers typesetting publication pages, but there is always the possibility that not all the text is copied over. There could be gaps where computer glitches have resulted in missed words, whole sentences, or entire sections. Worse, the copied text might have been corrupted when it was pasted into the new layout. On a related note, sometimes symbols and letters with accents do not carry across into the new software, or are scrambled on the way, so be especially wary of this kind of error when proofreading. Errors like these can be difficult to notice, so point to the need for particular attention to detail when proofreading. One tip is to check the word count of the text in the new layout. Is it what you expect it to be? If not, alarm bells should start ringing. The easiest way to ensure that the copy-edited text you submitted is what has arrived on the page is to check the proofs with the agreed text in front of you. That way, you will be able to see immediately if there are any deviations and you can flag them up for the designer or typesetter to put right.

Proofreading really does take time to get right. You are checking for all the areas we talked about in developmental and copy editing, to make sure that all aspects of the script are correct.

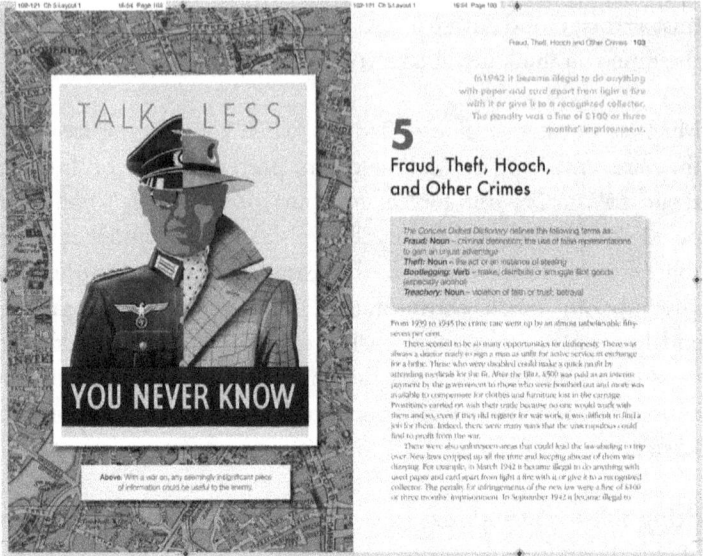

Original galley proofs for Crime in the Second World War: Spivs,
Scoundrels, Rogues and Worse' by Penny Legg

Some authors like to check their work several times, taking pains to check for specific points each time, such as style, format, spelling etc. Do not take anything for granted. I once left a telephone number in a text thinking it was something else entirely. I should have double-checked it, not assumed I knew what it was.

Nowadays, authors are often asked to proofread pdfs using a programme like Adobe Acrobat. This can seem daunting at the beginning but the advancing technology, and in particular, the ability of Acrobat to sync with the professional design programme InDesign via its Import PDF Comments option, means that authors can make changes to their script and these can then be downloaded directly into the typeset version of their work by the designer making the manuscript look great on the page. Depending on your version of Acrobat, which may vary, to access the editing software in Acrobat, open the pdf to be ready for editing and click the comments section in the options list on the right of the screen. This opens the commenting toolbar. Here are sticky notes, highlighters and text editing tools, such as replace text, strike through text and insert text. It is the edits made with the text editing tools that can be uploaded to InDesign.

Here are some tips to help you to proofread your work:

- To proofread competently, you need to be sharp-eyed to spot mistakes. Do not proofread when you are tired. You will regret it.

- Give yourself enough time to be thorough. If you rush, you will miss errors.

- Go through each chapter line by line, preferably reading it aloud.

- Ensure your fonts and their size are uniform throughout.

- Double-check all text in italics. This often does not carry over into design software.

- Check all images and their captions. Are the images in the right place and does each caption refer to the image on the page?

- Do not forget the front and end matter – is the Table of Contents listing accurate and complete? Do the page numbers correspond to the appropriate pages? Are the Acknowledgements, Foreword and Introduction in the right order? Is the Bibliography complete? Do all the website links work? Are all the pages listed in the Index correct?

- When proofreading the front and back covers, is the copy spaced correctly?

"I'll publish, right or wrong; Fools are my theme, let satire be my song."

English Bards and Scotch Reviewers (1809)
Lord Byron (George Gordon, 6th Baron Byron) 1788 - 1824
English Poet

Chapter 6
Understanding Different Publishing Models

At a time when there are more publishing options than ever before, every author needs to know and understand not just what is available, but the differences between each.

Early Publishing

In days gone by, authors wrote their manuscripts and then sought a publisher interested in either buying their work for publication or publishing it for a fee paid by the writer. If no publisher was interested, the book was either self-published or languished in a drawer never to see the light of day again. When you look at the history of publishing in this nutshell, it seems that little has changed.

Jane Austen (1775 - 1817) is known worldwide as a novelist whose works shed insight into the contemporary lives of women in a man's world. Her six full-length novels have never been out of print and have sold millions of copies in thirty-five different languages. Yet, she had to self-publish three of the four books that were published in her lifetime because she was either unable to interest a traditional publisher, or the publisher did not wish to take the risk of the book's failure. In 1797, her father, Rev. George Austen, wrote to Thomas Cadell the elder (1742 - 1802), a prominent bookseller and publisher, asking about publication of the manuscript *First Impressions*, which we know today as *Pride and Prejudice*. Cadell published well-known names, such as

Scottish poet Robert Burns, so asking him to publish a novel by an unknown female author was quite an ask. Her father's letter was returned, marked 'Declined by Return of Post.' (Le Faye, 2004, p. 104)

Today, many authors are in the same position. They aspire to publication, but how?

Traditional Publishing

A traditional publisher takes on the costs of publishing and marketing a book. A traditionally published author does not have to worry about the costs of editing work, cover or interior design, typesetting, publishing or printing. In return for allowing the publisher to publish the script, the author is paid via periodic returns on sales, known as a royalty, at a set percentage, sometimes with an advance of royalty paid at intervals before publication. The traditionally published author usually receives royalties twice annually after the advance has been repaid in book sales.

Major advantages to the traditionally published author are the fact that the traditional publisher will have distribution routes into bookshops and online retailers set up, will have networks with overseas publishing houses and so will have opportunities to sell rights to books for publication abroad, and will also usually have links to media outlets for book publicity. These areas can be difficult for the average author to enter. The publisher is discerning about which author to take on and many publishing houses will not entertain authors who do not have an agent representing them. This is because they will be inundated with scripts from eager would-be authors if they did not institute some kind of gatekeeping; only allowing those scripts through that have been judged worthy by a trusted and knowledgeable third-party.

Traditional publishers take the risk that the books they publish will do well. It is a finely balanced decision as to whose script to back and how much marketing budget to plough into it. Often, traditional publishers will take outside considerations into account when coming to a decision about whose work to publish. If the author has a large following on social media, for example, or is a well-known personality, there is more chance of clinching a deal than someone who is less well known or without a social platform.

Publishers want a quiet life, so an author with a track record of discord may well find it difficult to find a traditional publisher. They want an author they can work with, not continually battle.

It can be difficult to find a traditional publisher to take on a new author. Sometimes, the author is simply unlucky. Perhaps the target publisher has just taken on a similar project and does not wish to have two books on the same theme. There is little the author can do about this apart from try another publisher.

For those authors who get through the submission process, it can be a mixed blessing. Royalty payments can be as low as five per cent on net receipts, which, for example, means that a 200-page A5 size (148 x 210 mm or 5.8 x 8.3 inches) paperback retailing for £9.99 might bring in only £0.15 a copy for the author after all other costs have been accounted for, including the discount all retailers demand to stock the book on their (virtual) shelves. This discount can vary from 30 to 70 percent but averages out at about 40 percent. All authors these days are expected to help with the marketing of their publication and for some this can be a shock as they realise that there is a lot of hard work involved in interesting an audience in a new book. Some traditionally published authors will find that their book is well published and widely distributed, with the resulting financial reward making all the effort worthwhile. Others will end up with a nicely produced book but few sales, meaning a degree of disappointment. A few will wonder why they did not self-publish and by-pass the traditional publisher completely.

Tips to help find and work with a traditional publisher:

- Research publishers via *The Writers' and Artists' Yearbook* or a similar publication, and then look them up online.

- Target only publishers who take on the kind of book you have written. Believe me when I say that no publisher will step out of their chosen genres for your work, regardless of its merits.

- Follow the published submission guidelines to the letter.

- If you are offered a publishing contract, read it carefully. The Society of Authors in the UK or The Authors Guild in the USA both offer a contract vetting and advice service, which is comprehensive, so if you are not sure about what you are being asked to sign, contact one of these organisations.

- Do not accept the offer immediately. Think about it and only proceed if you are sure it is the best available.

- Suggestions for changes to your script will usually be made for specific reasons. Discuss these with your publisher to find out why they are being suggested before making a decision to accept or reject them.

- Be prepared to compromise.

Agents

Sometimes, the lack of an agent is the sticking point when trying to find a traditional publisher.

Agents negotiate on behalf of the authors they take under their wing. They know what publishers want and can usually spot a winner when they see one. They want the best for their author and are skilled in bargaining for the sale of rights to their author's work for an agreed price.

Joining an agent's list can be difficult. Agents earn roughly 15 per cent of any deal they broker for the author (paid by the author, not the publisher), but nothing if they do not achieve an agreement. This makes them super-critical about any work sent to them because their livelihood depends on their making correct decisions.

Some tips for finding an agent:

- An online search for agents will yield many agency profiles. Look at the genre they list as being of interest and contact only those who work in your area. It is a waste of time, for example, writing to an agent who works with science fiction authors, if your work is a biography.

- You have more chance of securing an agent if you look for new agents looking to build their list.

- Research the authors your target agent works with. Do you fit in? If not, look for another agent.

- Contact them by name. If you address your covering letter to 'Dear Sir or Madam' you will not get far!

- Follow any submission guidelines to the letter.

- Network widely to meet agents and those who might be able to help you find representation. Joining LinkedIn can help here. This social media platform is for professionals and is useful for business networking.

Self-Publishing

For those who cannot find a traditional publisher, or who make the conscious decision to go it alone, self-publishing can be a useful option. The explosion of self-publishing choices can make this seem attractive, particularly when companies like Amazon offer royalty payments of between 30 and 70 percent on sales. This is likely to be far more than the traditionally published author is offered but it is important to realise that for this the author has to do all the work; pay for everything along the way, and take the risk that after considerable effort, the book may not sell. Costs can be substantial when you take into consideration that it is the author who pays for the ISBN and legal deposit obligations, editing, the cover design, typesetting, publishing, printing and marketing. With the self-publishing model, the author pays all the costs and takes all the risks but does reap all the rewards, giving none to the middleman.

Print-on-demand (POD) and e-book publishing has made self-publishing more affordable and, these days, only the optimistic or the gullible end up with a garage full of print books. POD means just that; a book is only printed when an order for it comes in. This means that it is cost-effective to print just one copy of a book if that is all that is requested. In the case of e-books, there are most of the print publication costs, minus printing, but still the major costs associated with putting the book together, such as editing and designing the cover.

A self-published author needs to understand that all marketing efforts are down to them. If they do not have a marketing plan, the book will probably not find its audience. Book sales do not magically happen. There has to be some effort put into advertising and marketing.

Self-publishing can be both fulfilling and mentally tiring. It can be the culmination of a dream to see your book in print for readers to enjoy, but it can also be a headache to get to that point, with, for example, problems in formatting a script to the different e-book platforms causing some authors much stress. The costs involved can be off-putting for many authors, too.

There are a myriad of companies willing to help authors self-publish. Many are reputable but some are not, so all authors contemplating hiring a self-publishing company should read the small print carefully. As in so many things in life, a recommendation from a trusted source is often a safer way to go.

Here are some tips to help you to self-publish successfully:

- Invest in professional editing and design. Sadly, a self-published book often stands out because of its lack of quality.

- Ask questions. Ensure you know exactly what you are going to get when you sign an agreement.

- Do not rush!

- Amazon and its Kindle Direct Publishing (KDP) may look attractive, but research this platform thoroughly before making a decision. If you publish through this company, you may find that you cannot publish your book anywhere else, for example on Kobo, Apple etc. Amazon is refining its publishing offering all the time, so make sure to check out the latest information online.

Vanity Publishing

The so-called Vanity Publisher will print anything they are asked to print, regardless of its quality. They will not edit it or offer advice on the script. They will produce a book for a price, often a high price, and will frequently offer seemingly handsome discounts for bulk purchases of the resulting book. Some authors are happy with the results of their vanity-published book, others end up with something that is not saleable and which quietly yellows and ages with hundreds of its fellows in the author's garage, spare room, or storage container.

Vanity publishers are fine if you would like, for example, a thousand printed copies of an edited manuscript and you are happy to have it printed and bound for a price. Bear in mind though, that if you are in this situation, you could go to a printer to do the same job, probably for a considerably cheaper price. In both circumstances, you will be left to do all marketing and distribution.

Partnership Publishing

The Partnership Publisher is usually an ethical company whose owners have seen the gap between the traditionally published and the self-published author. You may sometimes hear these companies referred to as Hybrid Publishers or Fee-Per-Service Publishers, as they offer a mix of the best service choices from both traditional and self-publishing. A partnership publisher works with the author and will usually offer a range of publishing options as they realise that one-size does not always fit all. Thus, the author who has written their memoirs for their family might approach a partnership publisher to have their book edited and produced to a professional standard but might not want it made available for sale commercially as they might just want a few copies for members of their family. Another author might have an edited script, but it needs a front cover, and the writer wants commercial publication, and distribution. A third might have a script but will need a full professional service, from developmental editing of the work through to marketing the finished product. As you can see from these examples, partnership publishers work with a wide range of authors in different circumstances.

A partnership publisher, such as Sabrestorm Stories, the publisher of this book, will discuss with the author their needs and wants, and then try to find options to suit those areas identified. This may include editing, cover design and typesetting, in addition to publishing and printing. It will also go further and may offer services such as author coaching, marketing advice, legal deposit of the published books in deposit libraries and distribution. The author pays for the services they receive but is secure in the knowledge that they are only paying for what they need, and will, in return, know that the product, whether it be a print book, an e-book, or both, will be the best it can be, just as it would be if the book had been published traditionally. Partnership publishers are often smaller publishing houses than many of the traditional companies some authors may find intimidating, and they pride themselves on working very closely with their clients so that they know exactly what is required.

Some partnership publishers go further still and offer full management and distribution of the book once it is published. This will usually be for a fee or a share of the royalties. There is much debate within the writing community about the concept of sharing royalties between the author and the publisher. Sadly, some hybrid publishers have been accused of malpractice in this area, particularly if the author is asked to sign away their rights to their work. As with most things, it is best to read contracts, ask questions and take advice before entering into agreements, regardless of the terms.

If an author is interested in the royalty share option, the advantage is that the author does not have to keep track of all the various outlets the book might be sold from, including overseas sales, and will receive a periodic statement detailing all the sales made, together with a payment, similar to the way that traditional publishers deal with their authors. The royalty rate in a shared royalty situation (often between 40 and 60 per cent) is often much higher than a traditionally published author would be offered (often between 5 and 15 per cent) and this is shared equally between the author and the publisher. The publisher in this case also has a vested interest in promoting the book, so may also work closely with the author to assist with or support the author's marketing plans. They may also enter the book into trade guides, such as those offered in the UK by *The Bookseller*, which book retailers use to decide what to stock in the coming seasons. In this case, the author does not control the publishing account, which some authors may see as a disadvantage because they want to control all aspects of their work and receive all the income from their book.

Some partnership publishers offer a service whereby they offer all the needed options for bringing the book to publication, editing, design, cover etc. and then set up the publishing accounts on behalf of the author. They then hand the login details to the author and stand back, allowing them to take over the running of the publishing accounts. This model sees the author retaining all the royalties the book makes (often between 40 and 60 per cent), after the usual costs. This option can be attractive to authors who are happy to take over the running of their publishing account and who wish to receive all the income from their book. Depending on the publisher, this may be the end of the relationship between the two. Some offer onward support in terms of marketing and publicity but others do not.

Partnership publishing is a very subjective area, and it is up to the individual to decide which way to go. If they trust the publisher to manage their onward publishing account as well as they managed the editing, design and production phases of their title, and if they want the security of knowing someone else is minding their account, then paying for the company to continue to manage the publishing account might make sense. If, however, the author feels competent to manage all the various publishing streams, then receiving their account details may be the way forward for them. As always, it is best to discuss the options with the company and to take independent advice before signing on the dotted line. A recommendation is often worth much when it comes to deciding on whether to work with a partnership publisher and which model to choose.

Here are some tips for finding and working with a partnership publisher:

- Be prepared for a long-term relationship with your partnership publisher, particularly if they manage the publishing account for your book.

- A reputable partnership publisher will want to talk to you to ensure that they are the right option for you.

- An ethical partnership publisher will not publish your script if they do not think it is up to scratch and will work with you to help you to make it the best it can be. This may involve more cost to you, especially if your script is not complete until after you have agreed a publishing package. If the resulting script is not thought to be viable, an ethical publisher will refund your payment.

- Never sign a contract for services with a partnership publisher without talking to the company and seeing some of their products. There are many partnership publishers and some of them can be confused with vanity publishers, who will print a shopping list if you pay them enough!

- Be prepared to pay for the services you receive. A reputable partnership publisher will itemise each service in writing, so you know exactly what you are buying.

"Ensure that your target publisher is actually accepting submissions!"

Penny Legg, Author and Publisher

Chapter 7
Submitting Your Work for Publication

Submission Guidelines

If you have written a book, article, poem, or short story that you wish to submit for publication, there are usually guidelines to follow, issued by the target publisher. These are not in place for fun. They are there to ensure that submissions are in a format that is convenient for the publisher. The guidelines will cover basics like layout and font, and will ask for specific sections, such as a synopsis, covering letter and, if appropriate, the script or part of it. In the old days, when everyone submitted their work via snail mail, there were rules about paper and font colour, too. All of these add up to a set of guidelines for the writer that lead to a uniform submission for the recipient, thus making it easier for a fair evaluation of the work. Publishers know what they want and writing the guidelines will, they hope, ensure they get it.

So, where does this leave the writer? Well, in many ways, these guidelines are good things as they take the guesswork out of submitting. A writer knows by reading them exactly what is needed, how it should be formatted for the publisher and how it should be sent in. The author can then put the submission together without the stress of wondering if they are getting it right, and worrying that they might not.

Submission guidelines have another purpose, too. They separate those who follow rules from those who do not. Publishers, by and large, want a quiet life, just like most of us. They are usually inundated by eager authors, all convinced that their work is perfect. There are often many more manuscripts than there are spaces in publishers' lists, on magazine or newspaper pages or within anthology compilations. There must be a simple mechanism to make an initial sift in order that those who survive this can be given priority attention. Put simply, those who do not follow the submission guidelines are the first weeded out. The delete key is very handy in a technological age! In days gone by, the pink paper or green ink of a rogue paper submission stood out, exactly as the writer intended. This made it easy for the manuscript to be thrown in the rubbish bin for not conforming. Nowadays, when most publishers refer to 'typescripts', and few like to receive hard copy submissions, a writer who ignores guidelines is likely to be judged hard to work with. If they cannot follow simple rules at the beginning, they are out. Publishers, more often than not, will not want to waste precious resources on someone who makes their life difficult.

Here are some tips for submitting your work for publication:

- Check to see if there are submission guidelines.

- Read them diligently!

- Follow them to the letter!

- Give the publisher exactly what is asked for, no more or less. Let the brilliance of your work stand out, not the colour of your font.

Submitting for Publication

I was lecturing at a well-known writing conference a few years ago. The class was full of authors desperate for tips on how to make a good impression when submitting their work for publication. I decided to show them some real examples of covering letters, manuscript submissions, and authors' reactions to their rejection letters.

It was obvious from some embarrassed sniggers that a selection of my audience had written a covering letter starting: 'Dear Sir or Madam' or, 'To Whom It May Concern.'

This laziness in not researching the name of the correct person to address their letter to meant that the whole submission had been a waste of effort.

The biggest reaction, laughter, was to the following quote, from an author after reading the reject slip.
'I can't understand it! I know they said black ink and Times New Roman font for my manuscript, but everyone's submission looks like that, so how would they notice mine? I thought my green type looked great!'

"Publishers often do not have the resources to build an author up into a star."

Penny Legg, Author and Publisher

Chapter 8
Author Branding and Book Marketing

I recently received an email from an author who was lamenting the fact that her books were not selling. "I am hopeless online and at self-publicising, so am selling a few copies at a time at local craft fairs. Hard work!" she said.

The book world has changed. Just a few years ago, the print media, I mean newspapers and magazines, were the primary source of information about authors. They were interviewed and the resulting article, together with a photo, would appear in a periodical, often linked to the launch of their latest book and an appropriate anniversary or other buying hook. Publishers had publicity teams for their authors. They hunted out opportunities for launches, book signings, author talks and the like. Publishers were discerning about their publishing contracts but were more likely to take a chance on a new author if they liked their manuscript and thought they were worth fostering.

Today, we have the digital age. Traditional publishers have had their operating models disrupted by the advent of e-books, self-publishing, and Amazon, making them more cautious about the authors they contract and how much to spend on marketing. Newspaper circulations have declined, meaning there is less scope for promotion in hardcopy, although most have an online presence. Social media and blogs now spread information to an eager audience, hungry for new content and to know more about who writes it.

Readers are still out here, but they read in different ways. Some want physical books and magazines, but many want the convenience of digital, meaning they have access to their library anywhere. Increasingly, too, it is to online sources that readers turn to research who and what to read, as the popularity of Goodreads shows.

What this means is that authors need to think about their branding at the same time as they are writing their manuscript. Big, traditional publishers, with eyes firmly on the bottom line, are often offering publishing contracts to those with a large social media and/or popular following. Many have lost their publicity department in an effort to stay afloat in lean times and so do not have the resources to build an author up into a star. The author has to do this for themselves. Many people self-publish, thinking to bypass rejection, and hope that once the book is out, it will, by some miracle, sell. Consequently, as my correspondent demonstrates, many authors find out the hard way that selling books is about more than having good content.

Branding Basics

In short, authors need to have at least the basics in place when they submit manuscripts, regardless of whether this is to a traditional or a hybrid publisher, or if they wish to self-publish.

Publishers, and readers, check for a web presence. If they do not find one, the author is less likely to be taken seriously. A website does not have to be all-singing and all-dancing, or expensively produced. A simple page with a bio, a high-quality author photograph, a book cover with a short synopsis and contact details will suffice to begin with. If the author has a newsletter, then an opt-in form should also be included (with, perhaps, a free gift for opting in, known as a lead magnet). An online search for website providers turns up hundreds of hits, some of them with free design and hosting. Or, for those with less DIY confidence, a web designer who will put a simple site together is a good investment.

A blog is useful to discuss the progress of a book, announce its launch and to talk generally about what life is like as an author. It is a great platform to interact with your readers. Blogs are free and easy to set up via services such as blogger.com and wix.com, or any number of others offered from an online search. The blog and the website should be linked together so readers can click between the two.

Social media sites, such as Facebook, X (formerly Twitter), Tik Tok and Instagram, can be loud and crowded, which may be off-putting to the beginner. There are millions of people interacting on them, however, so an author should have an account for at least one of these sites, too. Facebook, for example, has roughly 3.07 billion users (DemandSage, 2025), so the potential audience is huge. Instagram specialises in visual content and is an online shopping centre, with visitors just waiting for news about the author and their work. Short X posts or Tik Tok videos are engaging. Each enables networking with readers on a grand scale, which allows an author to display authenticity and credibility. Put together, these social sites also allow publishers, journalists, and other thought leaders to gauge whether the author is worth taking notice of.

LinkedIn is a resource underrated by many authors. This social media site for professionals is the place to show off your status as an author. It is also a great place to build useful, lasting relationships with influencers. LinkedIn is the place to find journalists, photographers, book reviewers, those needing speakers, book shop staff and others who are looking for your expertise. By interacting on this site, you are displaying your worth as an author.

Depending on the author and how much time they wish to spend on establishing their online presence, all, or any, of these can build the author's brand. Your branding says a lot about you so choose what you say about yourself with care. Remember, though, in this era, an author needs to be visible to have a chance of success.

Here are some tips for successful author branding:

- Do not be tempted to use a quick snap as your author photograph. If there is anything sticking out of your head, reject the image!

- A clear head and shoulders photograph taken in a relaxed pose is the best option but make sure it does not look like a prison mugshot!

- You do not need to spend a fortune to set up a website, although you will have to pay for a domain name and hosting of the site. Look for reputable suppliers, like Go Daddy, Wix, Word Press or Yahoo.

- When thinking about your domain name, try to get your own name, if possible. My site is www.pennylegg.com, for example. You might have more than one book, so having a site in the book title, which many authors do, is of less use with multiple books. If you have a company name or run a training programme linked to the book, the option of having a website in the company or programme title is also useful. Think about how your reader will find you and go with the option that gives the most flexibility so that your reader comes straight to you.

- Be aware that taking on a social media profile is a commitment. Set aside time for it each day or appoint someone to do so on your behalf.

- If you are not sure about using a social media platform, look for an online guide. There are many to choose from. Learn how they work and what you can do with them before you set up your site.

Book Marketing

Of necessity, this short guidebook will only scratch the surface of the huge topic of 'Book Marketing'. There are many books and online resources to turn to when thinking in-depth about how to market your book. There are, though, some simple areas to consider when beginning to think about this topic.

The author at the start of this chapter had the right idea in that to sell books she found it helpful to interact directly with her audience. Readers like to engage with authors. If you think about it, many of us aspire to write a book. At some stage in our lives, we wonder if we might be able to write one. However, how many of us put pen to paper or fingers to keyboard and do so? Not so many. Of those who start, how many finish? Fewer still. Life is full of distractions. Of those who have a complete manuscript, how many finish with a published book? Only a handful. Many readers instinctively understand this and so look up to a published author, putting them on a pedestal simply because they went the distance, and they hold the proof in their hands. Opportunities to 'Meet the Author' are therefore sought out and these occasions can become cherished memories. When thinking about the marketing opportunities for your book, it is wise to consider the possibilities for meeting your readers and how you can offer your book when doing so.

Earlier in this chapter, I talked about the benefits of having an online presence to build a brand as an author. When thinking about marketing a book, many authors use their platforms to talk about the highs and lows of their author journey. Readers like to know insider information, so posts about happy, sad or funny events along the way build engagement that can then be used to advertise availability at in-person or online events where readers can meet the author in person.

Talking about, for example, rejected front covers can pave the way for a cover reveal to followers. This can be a fun and exciting event if handled well! Research conducted as part of the background for the book can be a useful topic to talk about, and, of course, pictures allow greater insight into the author's world, so take photographs you can post at every opportunity. Starting this interaction before the book comes out allows the author to build up a following of devoted fans ahead of the launch, each eager for the new book to come out.

When planning the marketing for a book, it is important to be realistic. Yes, in an ideal world it would be great to run a social media campaign covering all the platforms; to have Amazon and Google ads running before, during and after the book's (big) launch; to have a publicity agency championing you and to be at a series of public events, in-person and online, designed to bring your book to an interested public.

In reality, the average author needs to look at their circumstances and to know what constraints they have to work with. Do you have time (or inclination, or technical ability) to send out messages several times a week across all the social media channels? Or do you have the cash to pay someone to do this for you? Would you be better off choosing one platform and allocating time, an hour/ two hours/ whatever time you have each week to writing, scheduling and then posting messages? Do you have the money to run long-term online advertising for your book or would running short, cheaper advertising periods on the platform that holds the largest number of your potential readers work just as well – whether that be Amazon, Google, Facebook or somewhere else? Or should you forget paid advertising and spend your time writing authentic, targeted blog posts about all aspects of the book's research, writing, content and message? Do you have a publicity company to work for you? Can you afford one? If not, could you gather a team of people to help you with your publicity, or, in fact, to help you with all/any of the marketing of your book? It may be that you know people who can help. Ask yourself who you know and what they do. Would any of them be willing to help you in your book marketing journey? Recently, I was talking to an author who said that she had no one to help her. During our conversation, she realised that her husband had a colleague who used to work for a publisher in their marketing department and her son's girlfriend was a confident social media user. She asked them if they would help her and when they agreed, she had an instant marketing team! She was no longer alone with a seemingly daunting task. Spreading the project across a team is a confidence building exercise and can be fun, too, as you see things coming together.

So, saying all this, what are some key areas to think about when on your book marketing journey?

Six Months Before Launch

This is the time to think about your social media platforms, decide which you are going to work with, join them, start sending meaningful messages out and linking up with others.

Hire a website designer or start working on your website yourself. Decide on your lead magnet, which might be anything from exclusive, subscriber content, to something simple like a bookmark sent out via the postal service.

Have professional author photographs taken, ensuring that you buy the copyright to them so that you can use them commercially without having to pay the photographer for the right to do so.

Decide when and how you are going to launch your book. Some authors like to launch before publication, some on the day of publication and others after the book has been published. Some publishers offer copies of the book ahead of publication for review or sale at pre-launch events. Buyers are then encouraged to post early reviews. Some authors launch on the same day of publication. This can be risky as, if books are unavailable it will be embarrassing for the author. Some authors try to have at least two or three weeks between the book's release date and launch events. This will allow the book to be distributed and give time for early readers to write reviews. Regardless of when you decide to launch, you should consider these questions: Will you have a huge party in a smart hotel, with champagne and book readings, or will your launch be an intimate affair with just a few friends, family, and anecdotes? In practice, it will probably be something in between. I have launched books at large parties in hotels, clubs, museums and public houses; in gardens, libraries and at book shops; on a vintage bus and in the middle of a field! I have been interviewed during the launch event, given a talk with slides or video and have read excerpts from my books. I have always had books on sale and have been available to sign copies for readers. As you can see, there is no one way to launch a book! I always invited guests so that I knew how many were coming and could gauge the number of copies of the book I might need. Some authors sell tickets that include the price of the book, which is a good way to know precise numbers to order but does run the risk that asking for an upfront amount will put some people off coming. Whatever you decide to do to launch your book, now is the time to really think about what you want to do, how much it will cost, where and how you want to do it and then to start setting the details in place.

Decide on your paid advertising – what your budget will be, where you will advertise, how and when.

Four Months Before Launch

By now, you will have a following on social media so you should be sending out messages about how the book is progressing. If you have rejected covers, post about these in the run-up to a cover reveal, which is always an interesting post for followers. Just why did you decide on one rather than any of the others?

If you have been given marketing material by your publisher, now is the time to take it along to book shops, libraries, museums or anywhere else you think might like to stock the book. Have a conversation with the staff there and let them know about your book. If they are excited about it, they will be more likely to stock it.

Your website should be up and running by now, or very nearly ready. Don't forget to link your social media to it.

Your launch preparations should be well on the way to completion by now.

Six Weeks to Launch

Send out your launch invitations.

Keep talking about your book on social media.

Three Weeks to Launch

Celebrate the publication of your book – hooray! Congratulations.

Send out review copies to potential influencers, such as media editors, reviewers, book bloggers and podcasters. Don't forget to invite these people to your launch.

Be available for interviews.

Don't forget your social media posts.

Order copies of the book for your launch event(s).

If you have not already started your paid advertising, now is a good time to begin.

Launch Day

Have press releases and other marketing materials handy at the launch so that guests know your availability for interview as well as having concise information about the book.

Don't forget to take a pen to the launch! I speak from experience here – I had to stop at a supermarket to get a pen for my first launch because I had forgotten mine.

Have someone take photographs as they are great to use in marketing forever onwards.

Enjoy the event!

This list is by no means everything that you could do to market your book. Remember, book marketing goes on way after the launch, so you need to think about how you are going to continue the marketing into the future, too.

Here are some tips to help with marketing:

- If you think about your ideal reader and ask yourself what they want from you, it will be easier to look at the marketing possibilities for your book.

- A launch team can be composed of as many enthusiastic volunteers as you can find. List all the jobs you can think of that need to be done and then allocate them according to ability/availability amongst your team. Jobs can be as simple as posting a note to their email sign off about your book to reserving the launch venue on your behalf.

• Don't forget that online launches can be very effective! Have someone hosting so you do not have to do so and then talk about the book and read from it exactly as you might if you were running an in-person event. Book sales can be via paid ticket or by a link to your website or to Amazon or another retailer.

"There is an art of reading, as well as an art of thinking, and an art of writing."

Isaac D'Israeli (1766 – 1848) British Literary Historian (father of Benjamin D'Israeli, British Prime Minister 1868, 1874 - 1880)

Final Thoughts

The areas I have covered in this book are just some that confuse authors. I hope that you can see from what I have said that there are often many shades of grey in the writing and publishing world. As a rule, we all tend to look for a definitive answer in whatever we do, but in the sphere of written content there is often more than one avenue to tread. It is up to the individual writer to research, to ask questions and to take advice before deciding on the path that is best for them. This book is not meant to be the end of your investigations into which direction you should take, but the beginning. Armed with the tips I have given you, and the resources section that follows, my hope is that fewer authors will take decisions they later regret, or which cost them dear in terms of money, time or emotional toll.

I wish you happy writing and much publishing success.

Penny Legg

Glossary of Terms

A list of some of the common terms used within the writing and publishing world. This list is by no means exhaustive!

Advance: A Royalty amount paid to the author in advance, which then has to be earned back by book sales before the author receives any further payment.

Agent: Short for Literary Agent. A person who works for an author to sell their script to publishers.

Backlist: The titles an author has previously had published. They may or may not still be in print.

Book Fair: A gathering of publishing professionals for the purpose of buying and selling publishing rights. The biggest fair in the world is held in Frankfurt, Germany, usually in October each year. The London Book Fair is usually held annually in March.

ISBN: Acronym for International Standard Book Number, the number needed to identify your book and enable it to be listed for sale. A new ISBN is needed for each different version of your book, so, for example, the hard cover, paperback, and e-book editions of a title would all have different ISBNs.

Manuscript: This is literally a hand-written text but generally used nowadays for all typed submissions. Within publishing houses, this is sometimes referred to as 'typescript' these days.

Print on Demand (POD): Literally printing a book each time there is an order for it. This is an expensive way to publish in great numbers, but it does help to keep backlist titles, for example, or books on niche topics in print.

Proof: Short for galley proof, the typeset pages produced for final review before a book goes to press.

Royalty: The way authors are paid. A Royalty is a fee paid to an author based on sales of their book. It is usually a percentage of net sales. Royalties are traditionally paid twice yearly but, nowadays, can also be paid at other times, most notably monthly.

Slush pile: The name given to the unsolicited manuscripts publishers receive. Before digital submissions, authors sent hard copies to publishers, who literally stacked them in piles and read them when they had time to do so.

Wordcount: The number of words in a script.

Useful Resources

Organisations

Alliance of Independent Authors (ALLi) – an organisation dedicated to assisting independent authors to publish successfully.
www.allianceindependentauthors.org

Chartered Institute of Editors and Proofreaders – offers training and advice for and about editing and proofreading, including suggested rates for editing jobs.
www.ciep.uk

Fiverr – a place to find freelance professional help with areas such as website design and branding, amongst much else.
www.fiverr.com

Independent Publishers Guild (IPG) – supports independent publishers
www.independentpublishersguild.com

Jane Austen Literacy Foundation –
www.janeaustenlf.org

National Association of Writers' Groups (NAWG) – an organisation that helps to set up and run writing groups and which provides support for individual writers.
www.nawg.co.uk

Reedsy – an organisation that promotes freelance book editors, designers and marketers.
www.reedsy.com

The Authors Guild – the USA's professional organization for writers, aiding and protecting author's interest in copyright, fair contracts, and free expression since 1912.
www.authorsguild.org

The Society of Authors (SoA) – a Trade Union for authors. The SoA offers an excellent contract vetting service.
www.societyofauthors.org

Writers' Guild of Great Britain – a Trade Union for writers.
writersguild.org.uk

Books and Magazines

Eats, Shoots and Leaves – The Zero Tolerance Approach to Punctuation (London, Profile Books, 2003) by Lynne Truss – a simple to understand and very readable look at punctuation.

The Bookseller – the influential British book trade magazine, which publishes buyers' guides twice a year.
www.thebookseller.com

The Writers' and Artists' Yearbook (London, Bloomsbury Yearbooks, 2024) – a great resource for all authors and writers, offering a comprehensive listing of book and other media publishers, and a wealth of useful information for beginners to professionals.
www.writersandartists.co.uk

Writing Magazine – an excellent source of advice and
information for any writer
www.writers-online.co.uk

Writing & Publishing for Yourself: The Indie Author
Handbook, Self-Publishing Toolkit, and Staying Sane
Survival Guide: or 'The Adventures of an I.T. Helpdesk'
by Lisa Scullard (Createspace Independent Publishing
Platform, 2015) - a straightforward book of advice for all
authors wishing to self-publish.

People

Simon Whaley – author, journalist, editor, tutor
www.simonwhaley.co.uk

Bibliography

Aherne, M. and Baverstock, A. *The Naked Author - A Guide to
Self-Publishing* (London, A&C Black Publishers Ltd., 2011)

Le Faye, D. *Jane Austen: A Family Record.*
Second Edition. (Cambridge, Cambridge University Press,
2004)

Legg, P. *Crime in the Second World War: Spivs, Rogues, Scoundrels and
Worse* (Devizes, Sabrestorm Publishing, 2017)

About the Author

Penny Legg is the author of thirteen non-fiction titles, traditionally published by The History Press, The Thorn Press and Sabrestorm Publishing, covering local, military and World War Two history. She is also a journalist writing travel and history articles published in newspapers and magazines in the UK and abroad. She has written author advice articles for *The Link*, the magazine of the National Association of Writers' Groups (NAWG).

Penny is a member of the Society of Authors and the National Union of Journalists. In 2019, Penny and business partner Ian Bayley set up the partnership publishing company Sabrestorm Stories. This offers a range of publishing options to authors. She is an author coach for Sabrestorm Stories and for private clients. Penny has lectured widely in the UK and the USA. She is an accredited speaker with the Carnival cruise lines (Cunard and P&O) and for the Women's Institute. Penny lectures at the University of Portsmouth, working with mature students, and taught Business Writing at City, University of London. She was an Author Coach and the Publishing and Marketing Consultant for Capuccia Publishing in the USA. She has tutored for The Writers Bureau on their non-fiction, life writing and memoir, and editing and proofreading courses. She has worked with authors at all stages of their writing journey through charities and via Writing Buddies, the support group for writers.

Contact Penny via:
Website: www.pennylegg.com
www.linkedin.com/in/pennylegg
www.facebook.com/PennyLegg
Email: enquiries@pennylegg.com

If you found this book helpful, please leave a review online at your favourite literary website or online store.

About the Publisher

Sabrestorm Stories is a small, partnership publisher dedicated to producing beautiful books for authors who choose to work with industry professionals to bring their words to the public. Penny Legg and Ian Bayley founded the company in 2019 because they saw a gap in the provision for authors who either could not or did not wish to publish traditionally, but for whom self-publishing was daunting. Sabrestorm Stories offers bespoke publishing options for discerning authors with dreams of seeing their book in print, whether for their family or for a wider audience, in the genres of biography and memoir, self-help, general non-fiction and fiction.

Sabrestorm Stories' Services

Bespoke Partnership Publishing Services for Authors

- Author guidance

- Author branding

- Cover and interior design and layout

- Editing and proofreading

- Marketing support

- Publishing – print, ebook, special edition

If you would like an informal conversation to discuss your publishing dreams, please email:

enquiries@sabrestormstories.co.uk

Website: www.sabrestormstories.com